HEAD
OFF &
SPLIT

HEAD OFF & SPLIT

POEMS

NIKKY FINNEY

TriQuarterly Books/Northwestern University Press
Evanston, Illinois

TriQuarterly Books
Northwestern University Press
www.nupress.northwestern.edu

Printed in the United States of America

10   9   8   7   6

Library of Congress Cataloging-in-Publication Data

Finney, Nikky.
    Head off & split : poems / Nikky Finney.
      p. cm.
    ISBN 978-0-8101-5216-8 (pbk. : alk. paper)
    1. African Americans—Poetry. I. Title. II. Title: Head off and split.
PS3556.I53H43 2010
811'.54—dc22

                                             2010028888

To AJV

It's what you do

FOR LUCILLE CLIFTON

JUNE 27, 1936 ✝ FEBRUARY 13, 2010

Dahomey woman of light, laughter, language

Do not leave the arena to the fools.

—TONI CADE BAMBARA,
PHILADELPHIA, OCTOBER 1995

{postcard mailed from hospice bed}

CONTENTS

The Head · Waters

Veritas

ACKNOWLEDGMENTS

Every book I've ever written has found its way to its paper surface by way of the breath of the dead and the hands of the living. A long curtsy, crisp bow, and standing ovation to the Northwestern University Press team, Parneshia Jones, Marianne Jankowski, Jenny Gavacs, Serena Brommel, and other names I wish I knew to call; your brilliant, hard work is evident on every page. A. J. Verdelle, your editing prowess changed everything about this collection. Rachel Eliza Griffiths, through your lens the present and the future merge. Beulah L. Davenport, I am so grateful to you for teaching me how to look hard work and trouble in the eye. Ed Bradley, thank you for loving New Orleans out loud and choosing "Uncles" as your favorite poem. Bessie Coleman, you proved what we already knew: Black women are born to fly. Baby Lenora Kathleen Finney, birth and death date July 19, 1995: I still dream of you, long-legged, sweet sixteen this year, and a bookworm, of course. Lena Boxton and Claire Prymus, my best best girls who keep my oldest secrets. Iniva Ngaka, for your constant daughter-presence. Kenneth Newkirk, tender earth man, for your constant phone calls over the years. Marta Martinez for the firefly light of your friendship. Melynda and Baby James for the close community you make and nurture. To Kate Black, sublime cherry pie provider. To Chip and Jerry, my fine, fierce brothers. To Mama and Daddy whose fifty-five years of love remain my lighthouse. And to the two frolicking red foxes that greeted me one winter in the street at 4 A.M., reminding me of my affection for jubilee and wild.

The following poems have appeared in a slightly different form in the following publications: *PMS Journal*, "Cattails"; *Pluck! Journal of Affrilachian Life and Culture,* "Plunder"; *Lumina Journal,* "The Condoleezza Suite."

The Strom Thurmond and Modjeska Simkins quotes were found in *Strom: The Complicated Personal and Political Life of Strom Thurmond* by Jack Bass and Marilyn W. Thompson. They are used with permission of Jack Bass.

The Toni Cade Bambara quote is used with permission of Karma Bambara.

Gratefully, I bow.

HEAD
OFF &
SPLIT

Resurrection of the Errand Girl: An Introduction

The girl is sent for dinner fish. Inside the market she fills her aluminum bowl with ice-blue mackerel and mullet, according to her mother's instruction. The fishmonger standing there, blood on his apron, whale knife in hand, asks, Head off and split? Translation: Do away with the watery gray eyes, the impolite razor-sharp fins, the succulent heart, tender roe, delicate sweet bones? Polite, dutiful, training to be mother, bride, kitchen frau. Her answer, Yes.

Forty summers pass. Girl no longer girl. Her blood dries into powder red dust. It is the time of animals on the move: on land, fancy blue lights beep quotidian conversations deep into the inner ear of fast-walking humans; on thinning ice, polar bears turn cannibal and the last male emperor penguin is holding one solitary egg on the quivering slope of his webbed feet. In the oil-drenched Gulf a flotilla of grandfather sea turtles floats—shell down, feet up. On hurricane-soaked rooftops Black people have been abandoned—again. The errand girl, resurrected—woman, dutiful, grown—drives home as she often does to see the two who made her. On the way in, her mama calls, to ask if she can stop and pick up dinner from the market. Friday. Fish. Tradition as old as the South itself. An hour later, she steps into Liberty Street Market, this fragrant hundred-year-old fish house. Inside, the hungry wait wall to wall. Beneath her cotton dress she wears what she could not wear when she was the errand girl—her poet's gauzy slip. She pulls her chosen fish by the tail out of the bed of ice that anchors all sides of the room. She extends her full bowl of ice-blue mullet and flounder to the fishmonger-of-her-youth's son. A man her same age but of a different persuasion. He echoes the words he heard as a boy from his father, Head off and split? Her answer is offered even quicker than the fish. No. Not this time. This time she wants what she was once sent for left whole, just as it was pulled from the sea, everything born to it still in place. Not a girl any longer, she is capable of her own knife-work now. She understands sharpness & duty. She knows what a blade can reveal & destroy. She has come to use life's points and edges to uncover life's treasures. She would rather be the one deciding what she keeps and what she throws away.

She recognizes the fishmonger: he does not recognize her. Even though she is the daughter of the most beautiful woman in the world. He holds his inherited bone-handled whale knife high in the air, teasing her answer of refusal around. He laughs out loud, warning her about the painstaking work the toothy-bony fish will require. With his hairy hands around his own hairy neck he imitates choking on an overlooked bone. Nobody waiting in the fish market laughs. He is boastful, imprecise. Three Black boys wearing rubber aprons listen right behind him, waiting to be handed bowls of fish, for dressing. His backup chorus: three-dollar-an-hour, head-off-and-split boys, snugly set like rhinestones in the dark wet air behind him. They shine out in unison, their faces speckled with the white sequined scales of fish already beheaded. The boys honk a Pip-like reverie out into the salty air of the sweaty room. The sight and sound of them does nothing to change her mind. For once in her life she will not go sentimental. She will not rescind her order. She wants what she has come for kept whole, all marrow and every organ accounted for, just as it was pulled from the sea. Her whole fish is wrapped in yesterday's news, tied with white fishmonger string, and handed over. She steps through the crowd, slips out the door, heads home.

The Hard · Headed

Red Velvet

(for Rosa Parks, 1913–2005)

> People always say that I didn't give up my seat because I was
> tired, but that isn't true. I was not tired physically, or no
> more tired than I usually was at the end of a working day.
> No—the only thing I was—was tired of giving in.
>
> —ROSA PARKS

i

Montgomery, Alabama, 1955

The setting: A rolling box with wheels
The players: Mr. Joe Singleton, Rev. Scott,
      Miss Louise Bennett, Mrs. Rosa Parks,
      Jacob & Junie (fraternal twins, fourteen)

The game: Pay your Indian Head to the driver,
  then get off the bus.
  Then, walk to the door at the end of the bus.
  Then, reboard the bus through the Black back door.
  (Then, push *repeat* for fifty years.)

Sometimes, the driver pulled off,
before the paid-in-full customer
could get to the one open door.

Fed up with buses driving off—without them—
just as her foot lifted up, grazing, the steel step:

She was not a child. She was in her forties.
A seamstress. A woman devoted to
handmade things.

7

She had grown up in a place:
where only white people had power,
where only white people passed good jobs on
        to other white people,
where only white people loaned money
        to other white people,
where only white people were considered human
        by other white people,
where only the children of white people had new
        books on the first day of school,
where only white people could drive to the store
        at midnight for milk
        (without having to watch the rearview).

ii

A seamstress brings fabric and thread, collars & hems,
buttonholes, together. She is one who knows her way
around velvet.

Arching herself over a river of cloth she feels for the bias,
but doesn't cut, not until the straight pins are in place,
marking everything; in time, everything will come together.

Nine months after, December 1, 1955, Claudette
Colvin, fifteen, arrested for keeping her seat; before that,
Mary Louise Smith. The time to act, held by two pins.

iii

The Montgomery seamstress waits and waits for
the Cleveland Avenue bus. She climbs aboard,
row five. The fifth row is the first row of the Colored

section. The bus driver, who tried to put her off that day, had put her off twelve years before. But twelve years before she was only twenty-eight, still a child to the heavy work of resistance.

By forty-two, you have pieced & sewn many things together in segregated Alabama. You have heard "Nigger Gal" more times than you can stitch your manners down. You have smelled fear cut through the air like sulfur iron from the paper mills. The pants, shirts, and socks that you have darned perfectly, routinely, walk perfectly, routinely, by you. (*Afternoon. How do.*) Those moving along so snug in your well-made, well-sewn clothes, spit routinely, narrowly missing your perfectly pressed sleeve.

By forty-two, your biases are flat, your seams are inter-locked, your patience with fools, razor thin.

By forty-two, your heart is heavy with slavery, lynching, and the lessons of being "good." You have heard 7,844 Sunday sermons on how God made every woman in his image. You do a lot of thinking with a thimble on your thumb. You have hemmed 8,230 skirts for nice, well-meaning white women in Montgomery. You have let the hem out of 18,809 pant legs for growing white boys. You have pricked your finger 45,203 times. Held your peace.

iv

December 1, 1955: You didn't notice who was driving the bus. Not until you got on. Later you would remember, "All I wanted was to get home."

The bus driver, who put you off when you were
twenty-eight, would never be given the pleasure
of putting you off anything ever again. When he
asks you to move you cross your feet at the ankle.

Well—I'm going to have you arrested.

And you, you with your forty-two years, with your
21,199 perfect zippers, you with your beautiful
nation of perfect seams marching all in place, all
around Montgomery, Alabama, on the backs &
hips of Black & white alike, answer him back,

Well—You may go on and do so.

You are arrested on a Thursday. That night in
Montgomery, Dr. King led the chant, "There
comes a time when people just get tired." (He
wasn't quite right, but he was King.) He asked
you to stand so your people can see you. You
stand. *Veritas!* You do not speak. The indelible
blue ink still on your thumb saying, *Enough!*
You think about the qualities of velvet: strength
& sway. How mighty it holds the thread and
won't let go. You pull your purse in close,
the blue lights map out your thumb, blazing
the dark auditorium.

On Courthouse Monday, the sun day dew
sweating the grass, you walk up the sidewalk
in a long-sleeved black dress, your white collar
and deep perfect cuffs holding you high and
starched in the Alabama air. A trim black velvet
hat, a gray coat, white gloves. You hold your
purse close: everything valuable is kept near
the belly, just like you had seen your own mother

do. You are pristine. Persnickety. Particular.
A seamstress. Every thing about you gathered
up and in place. A girl in the crowd, taught not to
shout, shouts, "Oh! She's so sweet looking! Oh!
They done messed with the wrong one now."

You cannot keep messing with a sweet-looking
Black woman who knows her way around velvet.
A woman who can take cotton and gabardine,
seersucker and silk, swirl tapestry, and hang
boiled wool for the house curtains, to the very
millimeter. A woman made of all this is never to
be taken for granted, never to be asked to move
to the back of anything, never ever to be arrested.

A woman who believes she is worthy of every
thing possible. Godly. Grace. Good. Whether you
believe it or not, she has not come to Earth to play
Ring Around Your Rosie on your rolling
circus game of public transportation.

A woman who understands the simplicity pattern,
who wears a circle bracelet of straight pins there,
on the tiny bend of her wrist. A nimble, on-the-dot
woman, who has the help of all things, needle sharp,
silver, dedicated, electric, can pull cloth and others
her way, through the tiny openings she and others
before her have made.

A fastened woman
can be messed with, one too many times.

With straight pins poised in the corner
of her slightly parted lips, waiting to mark
the stitch, her fingers tacking,
looping the blood red wale,

through her softly clenched teeth
she will tell you, without ever looking
your way,

You do what you need to do &
So will I.

Left

Eenee Menee Mainee Mo!

—RUDYARD KIPLING, "A COUNTING-OUT SONG,"

IN *LAND AND SEA TALES FOR SCOUTS AND GUIDES*, 1923

The woman with cheerleading legs
has been left for dead. She hot paces a roof,
four days, three nights, her leaping fingers,
helium arms rise & fall, pulling at the week-
old baby in the bassinet, pointing to the eighty-
two-year-old grandmother, fanning & raspy
in the New Orleans Saints folding chair

Eenee Menee Mainee Mo!

Three times a day the helicopter flies
by in a low crawl. The grandmother insists on
not being helpless, so she waves a white hand-
kerchief that she puts on and takes off her head
toward the cameraman and the pilot who
remembers well the art of his mirrored-eyed
posture in his low-flying helicopter: Bong Son,
Dong Ha, Pleiku, Chu Lai. He makes a slow
Vietcong dip & dive, a move known in Rescue
as the Observation Pass.

The roof is surrounded by broken-levee
water. The people are dark but not broken. Starv-
ing, abandoned, dehydrated, brown & cumulous,
but not broken. The four-hundred-year-old
anniversary of observation begins, again—

Eenee Menee Mainee Mo!
Catch a—

The woman with pom-pom legs waves
her uneven homemade sign:

Pleas Help   Pleas

and even if the *e* has been left off the *Pleas e*

do you know simply
by looking at her
that it has been left off
because she can't spell
(and therefore is not worth saving)
or was it because the water was rising so fast
there wasn't time?

Eenee Menee Mainee Mo!
Catch a— a—

The low-flying helicopter does not know
the answer. It catches all of this on patriotic tape,
but does not land, and does not drop dictionary,
or ladder.

Regulations require an *e* be at the end
of any *Pleas e* before any national response
can be taken.

Therefore, it takes four days before
the national council of observers will consider
dropping one bottle of water, or one case
of dehydrated baby formula, on the roof
where the *e* has rolled off into the flood,

(but obviously not splashed
loud enough)

where four days later not the mother,
not the baby girl,
but the determined hanky waver,
whom they were both named for,
(and after) has now been covered up
with a green plastic window awning,
pushed over to the side
right where the missing *e* was last seen.

> *My mother said to pick*
> *The very best one!*

What else would you call it,
Mr. Every-Child-Left-Behind.

Anyone you know
ever left off or put on
an *e* by mistake?

Potato   Po tato e

     In the future observation helicopters
will leave the well-observed South and fly
in Kanye-West-Was-Finally-Right formation.
They will arrive over burning San Diego.

     The fires there will be put out *so well.*
The people there will wait *in a civilized manner.*
And they will receive *foie gras* and *free massage*
for all their trouble, while their houses don't
flood, but instead burn *calmly* to the ground.

The grandmothers were right
about everything.

People who outlived bullwhips & Bull
Connor, historically afraid of water and routinely
fed to crocodiles, left in the sun on the sticky tar-
heat of roofs to roast like pigs, surrounded by
forty feet of churning water, in the summer
of 2005, while the richest country in the world
played the old observation game, studied
the situation: wondered by committee what to do;
counted, in private, by long historical division;
speculated whether or not some people are surely
born ready, accustomed to flood, famine, fear.

My mother said to pick
The very best one
And you are not   it!

After all, it was only po' New Orleans,
old bastard city of funny spellers. Nonswimmers
with squeeze-box accordion accents. Who would
be left alive to care?

My Time Up with You

[A rickety porch somewhere in east Texas.]

the   air   is   calamity

The TV camera steadies against the wind, shining
the only good light left on the old woman's face.

Ain't going nowhere. Ain't moving. Not from this house.

The young man does not drop head or microphone.

Go save somebody else. Everybody at 621 already saved.

With her cane she points to the bright orange house numbers.
The young reporter does not speak. The sheriff deputy's
face is ruddy, puffing. He is nearly eating his car radio;

We ARE trying to get out. Roger, we are trying to get out now! Over.

The young "tom brokaw" situates the camera on her face.
Mayree Monroe is chewing down an old bone, taken out
of her mama's mouth. A bone that won't go down.

You say Rita coming? Well, she just gonna have to come on.

Miss Monroe hands the sky everything in her pockets.

Come on Rita girl. Come on gal, get yourself on Mayree's list.

Her eyes & words fall to Mr. Tall Handsome, camera-
keeping up with her every move;

Iss gonna be me and Rita tonight, Baby!

He hoists the great silver eye off his shoulder. Looking
behind, on guard to the loud laughing wind. No time.
He's got to make her understand.

One hour ago when they arrived for this little
human-interest story, he didn't think it would
take this long. How could it take this long? All
up and down the street: Whipping clotheslines.
Spanking trash cans. Snapping live wires.
Twenty-foot vaulted trees. Downspouts playing
steel pan with the trembling ground. Every wild
thing prone to stillness now. Miss Monroe's screen
cracks then pops. The top hinge lunges wild, free.

*Miss Monroe, please come with us, everybody has been
evacuated—but you. We need to get in the car now and go.
We really need to go. If we leave without you no one will
come back for you—not even when you change your mind.*

He means well. He has a kind voice. Wearing
those You Can Trust Me I Served In The Peace
Corps eyes. He has seen the inside of a church
twice, walking all the way to the front both
times, surprising even his mother as he dropped
to his knees.

The old woman, three times his age, points, then
claps her hands like a much younger woman.
When she does her top teeth shift, slip. She stands.
Using both hands she smoothes down the cotton
fabric from hipline to another invisible mark just
above her knee. She does this in one fluid motion.
This is the oldest signal in the Western Hemisphere
between an old Black woman and whosoever
her company happens to be.

My time up with you her standing-up legs and
smoothing-down hand signals say. But the young
"tom brokaw" has not studied his field guide
to Black women.

With help of the feral wind Mayree Monroe comes
to her highest height. He continues to pan & zoom,
finding the strip of duct tape holding crooked the
one arm of her black-rimmed glasses. She kisses
her fingers then waves to his curvy green glass third
eye. Imitating the long-legged Black girls from the
Ebony Fashion Fair, found in her monthly *JET*
magazine, she arcs her thin arms toward the giant
orange 621, newly painted and still drying on the
front of her house. Before the deputy arrived,
while Oakland Road piled into SUVs & flatbeds,
with engines still running, Mayree Monroe hunted
for her paintbrush.

She turns and walks inside her shotgun house,
pushing and latching the screen door so hard
until the picture of her wavy blond Redeemer
goes wavy—shakes, but does not fall. The camera
keeps churning. The old woman starts her roll
call, using her fingers to count. The patrol lights
on the Sheriff's car twirl in front like the vehicle
that has come to escort a person of importance
to the County Fair, where once in their seats,
all will hear the cigar-laced midget ring out:

Come and See the Disappearing Lady!
Here one minute gone the next!

I told you, the deputy says to "tom brokaw,"
'hit was the same as this morning. She named
every last one she's lived through. David '79.

19

Charley '80. Norma '81. *She give the name and*
the year perfect. Bonnie '86. Gilbert '88. Arlene '93.
Bret '99. Claudette '03. *Name and year, one by one.*

The young "tom brokaw" zooms in and frames
the 621. He quickly brings the camera down.
The engine is running. Mayree Monroe has shut
her door in his face. Both of the deputy's feet
are in the car tapping the sopping floor mats.
Boards and metal siding fly then tumble down
the street. Young "tom brokaw" does not turn
his back to her. His eyes flutter, up and around
every missing nail and dangling soffit in sight.
For the third time in his life he is back on his
knees. He backs his way to the car lowering his
camera to the seat. His cheeks are not as dry
as the skittish lawman's. He slides his boots in,
his body fights his mind & knees—then follows.

The Texas dust is laid down.

Through the thin laminated door he hears
Mayree Monroe latching her three deadbolts.
The two-by-four that her nephew, Jimmy, cut &
nailed for added protection, is squeezed down
& over iron brackets bolted into the wall.
It is the same as any other night. Alone, finally,
with her wavy-haired Redeemer.

> *Master of Man, where they gonna send Mayree Monroe?*
> *I already got me a house. What's a Superdome anyway?*
> *What kind of a name is U-tah? U-tah don't sound nice*
> *as Texarkana. Rent free, they quick to say.*

She shakes her fist. The blinding rain is now flooding
every street for thirty miles in every direction. All phone

lines are down now. Lights, out now. She searches a
wooden drawer for a match to light her grandmother's
cobalt blue kerosene lamp.

> *Never give me nothing free before. Now all of a sudden*
> *they handing out* Free! *like butter or jumbo packs of Juicy*
> *Fruit. Sweet Redeemer, where does Mayree go when she has*
> *finally paid off her house and the mannish hurricane is*
> *thundering down?*

Mayree Monroe's hand is steady. She strikes her one
piney match in one praising stroke. The room blooms
around her with the shadows of her precious things.
A zephyr hits the porch so hard a marble hole happens
quick to the wall. She does not look.

> *I have paid off this house three times over what anybody*
> *else ever would've paid. Nobody at Community Savings*
> *& Trust thought I could do it.*
>
> *Just like nobody in that yard today believe I can make it*
> *through this night. Disbelief will run you straight into*
> *the arms of the Devil. My Sweet Redeemer.*
>
> *Lily of my Valley, "odds ain't the best" they say. Did you*
> *hear 'em talkin' to me that way?*

Dropping her voice down to a whisper, she stands like a
black beam against the wind, both arms akimbo.

> *Well, odds ain't never been the best*
> *for Mayree Monroe and her kind.*

Walking over to her rocker, she pulls the thin cushion
off the seat, weaving left arm over right arm, she straps
in for the night.

"Change my mind"? "tom brokaw" have the nerve to
shape his mouth and say. This Mayree Monroe,
of 621 Oakland Avenue, daughter of Ester Brown,
of 18 Clementine Road, granddaughter of Mary One,
of Route 4, Box 318. I will be here 'til the end.

Plunder

The president had his annual physical today. His heartbeat, at fifty-two beats per minute, is said to rival that of a professional athlete.

—JOHN SEIGENTHALER, NBC *NIGHTLY NEWS*

i

He has come to give his last State of the Union
address. He walks through the Great Hall, one
final presidential parade, touching those waiting
on both sides. A tumultuous welcome. His walk
in is exquisitely bipartisan. His annual moment
of public respect, last chance to make his case
to the American public without pokes from
pesky reporters. He can say what he wants, it's
live TV, then head home for the evening, eat
Stubbs bar-be-cue without being questioned,
sleep, a satisfied man. His blue tie is perfectly blue,
perfectly tied. His hair has grayed faster than any
president in modern history. The applause goes
on and on for ten minutes.

ii

On and on, the applause *loop de loops,* making a
political pep rally, a Washington tradition; what a
show! How very American, how very undivided
we are, how we promise on the hide of every
endangered polar bear, on the feather of every
balding eagle. Everything we think and do is

absolutely not made in China. The clapping hands
die as if ruled by baton. It's time—. He opens up
his brown folder. He takes longer than he should.
He looks up and finds the First Lady sitting beside
a woman in a gray burka. Women in Afghanistan
have rights now. He believes he is responsible for
this. On the other side of the First Lady is a large
German shepherd, the other war hero.

iii

The panting shepherd war hero being honored
gets a presidential wave. A high, lonesome, over-
the-top gesture, a cowboy-come-professional
athlete offering his last night under lights. He
imagines himself back in his boyhood chaps.
The First Lady seems shocked by her husband's
hyperbolic overture. Librarians and presidents
have references in common. Fingering her Dewey
Decimal hemline, she refrains from returning
his wave. The president coughs, jostling his papers.
Without warning he closes his executive leather-
ette, running his hand over the front, lightly.
Like most professional athletes he likes to stroke
& palm fine Texas cowhide.

iv

With his AAA Texas hide, the president rests his
left hand on his left hip, a move that resembles a
cowboy smacking a calf butt—the legs are tied.

He wipes his brow, then pockets his hanky while
awaiting his applause & scores. He has never really
smacked a calf on its butt, but there is a movie
theater inside the White House that he slips inside
of sometimes when the Oval Office closes down
for the night and he can't. With both wars raging
endlessly on, he's been staying up later than usual
to watch his numbers fall. Afterward, he feels well
briefed. His heroes smack buckshot on Indians.
He has a silly grin on his face. He likes being home
on the White House range.

v

Home on the range, a White House boy bucks
bad, the president, a C student with a pocketful
of money, and only one night before graduation.
With nothing to lose he slowly cocks his head
and loosens his tie with his free hand. A mystery
camera finds the secretary of state, whose fingers
have already dropped from checks to pockets,
where there, brown & classical, her fingers try to
wiggle their way back to the safety of a Steinway.
The chief of staff waves his hands wildly, not
realizing that the Great Hall records. A camera
is not supposed to be on him. The president of
the United States decides to make a wish.
Here goes:

vi

The president of the United States wishes he had
taken his rookie season more seriously and worked
on his fundamentals. Now his team is behind and
waiting around for the ball. He shakes his head.
I know, I know. You told me. Twice. Stick to the play-
book. He holds his soft well-oiled hands up in the
air. Faking a shot. *I remember.* The president's wrists
tremble. His eyes bat about more than normal.
His heart rate is fifty-two beats per minute. Longhorn
strong. Healthy. Prime time. Hardly uneasy. Not unsteady.
He's still very much a Texan, still a secret society
Yale man with strong blue-blood brother connections.
But it's nearing the end of his career, and there's
never been a half-court shot.

vii

The clock is ticking down and he's still far from
his Hail Mary. He looks into the camera, one eye
on the rope and the other on some handsome
imaginary steer. He dreams of the postgame,
back on the GH ranch, in Crawford, without
the sorority of protest mothers, one of whom
was removed from the building in wrist cuffs,
her son's face, breast high, painted neon yellow,
on her Fruit of the Womb, pearl white anti-
war T-shirt. The president's hand itches, ready,
at the lasso. He really wants to brand the family
B on the steer's butt. Sick of playing safe—
keeping to the ratty George Washington playbooks
given to him day one.

viii

He's honored every chapter of the GW playbooks.
He hasn't sent any body to the electric chair in
years. He never kept slaves like it says to do right
in chapter 1. He quit drinking. Hell—tonight's
the night. "Listen," he says, with more lone star
drawl, "some a ya'll think I haven't done much
right these last few years. I know my numbers
have dropped from Kansas to Kentucky. But hey,
I'm still your go-to guy. The clock shows two seconds
and the score's tied." He waves away the pleading
chief of staff and keeps on running down the court.
"So get this—I'm in the limousine riding sidesaddle
and that great American Dolly Parton is singing—
really talking to me."

ix

With Dolly singing deep in his ear he takes one
deeper breath shifting his weight to his good foot.
His handlers have not yet told him that James Brown
is dead. All the steers in Texas rush the room, poking
their heads in the door. "So Miss Dolly wrote this
song back in '93, said it this way, 'Ain't it funny
how the years will find you searching through your
plunder looking for all the treasures you gave up?'
Now ain't that a song worth singing!" He laughs
a big ole Texas-size laugh, slaps his hip, and shakes,
rattles, then slow rolls his head. His laugh is his
greatest accomplishment—in eight long years.
Most of the steers standing around just don't get it.
The secretary of state hits a high note. *Crescendo.*

x

Repeats. This crescendo, in F major. Lip-syncing
the words better than Milli Vanilli. He palms the
ball again like he really wants to keep shooting.
He knows he should pass but it's the end. It is
midnight of every muscle-hearted wannabe.
Game over & out. With his right hand he fakes
a pass, then imagines a beautiful Michael Jordan
follow-through. His wrist hangs in the air like a
frozen praying mantis. He's feeling Dolly deeper.
"So true, Mr. President, so true!" a loyal fan
shouts. "My fellow Americans—Ain't it funny how
the years will find you searching through your plunder—
looking for all the treasures you gave up." *Treasures?*
Plunder? Get it? Well, are you with me?

xi

In his plundering mind—everyone is with him.
He takes off streaking. Down court. President
#43 of team United States stretches out his
hands, the nets swish, end to end, in the great
Republic of America Center. He sweeps his
hands up near his head. He is stupefied at his
luck, his skill. He turns, mouth open, fleeing
up and down the court. The crowd going wild,
screaming around him. He checks the clock,
his sneakers squeak to a halt on the parquet floor,
the Capitol building quiets. Gathering the corners
of his jacket collar, GQ, he rests his hands on
his leather hips, waiting for the pretty sports
lady with the pretty microphone.

xii

The pretty sports lady with matching microphone
never arrives. The postgame interview with the
One who made it all happen never happens. The
big clock is out of time. The president concedes.
"Well, God bless Dolly Parton and God bless
America." The president of the United States
salutes the screen as he offers the camera a big
ole Texas-size championship smile. The air in the
Great Hall is still. The Dolly-Parton-State-Of-The-
Union address is now history. #43 closes down
the fine-grain black cowhide cover, over the perfect-
ly aligned, never read, pages. He doesn't pick them
up or carry them away. He knows another will
come behind him and pick up his mess.

xiii

Somebody always picks up his mess, so he leaves
detritus—pole to pole. He turns and shakes the
hand of the VP and the majority whip. He walks
down to the floor of the Great Hall, back the
same way he came. The camerawoman is in a
quiet spin, wondering, will somebody in the
control booth cut away for a commercial like they
did for Kanye West the night of the Katrina tele-
thon, when Kanye didn't follow the script either.
But nobody cuts. The Joint Chiefs of Staff are
silent. The House of Representatives is stunned.
The Senate, fidgeting. The VP has managed, hand
over heart, to slip out a side door. The main camera
is fixed on the rostrum. The final game. Finally over.

xiv

It's over, so over. The air that had been electric,
is now flat, limp, popcorn strewn. No time left
on the clock. Only time now to raise the always
perfectly blue tie to the rafters. The presidential
exit is high Washington tradition. All the steers
are standing, chewing their cuds. The Speaker of
the House, who always sits behind the president
during the State of the Union game, now holds
his heavy chin in his even heavier hands. The two
new Supreme Court justices reach to shake the
president's hand. The justices don't know what
else to do. The all-star cabinet bobbles, bubbles,
surrounding him like a great body of water.
Tadpoles squirming at the silky shore.

xv

At the shore of something monumental and dry-
ing up, the president of the United States walks
out through the Great Hall to polite adulation
& steady applause. His blue tie is alarmingly blue.
His hair has continued graying, and is now quick-
silver rich. It's a long walk out. Another proud
fan cups his hand and shouts, "You tell 'em 43!"
The president hears his sweetest name called,
turns, smiles, and waves. It is a big ole Texas-size
wave. Cheerleader women & Secret Service men
turn and disappear behind the president. He feels
he has delivered the goods. Now he will hum Dolly's
Plunder all the way back to the White House.
He is drenched, spent. He feels real real good.

xvi

He is all feel goody and Dolly-soaked. He has
finally shed the wool of the privileged son and
grown the skin of the thinking ballplayer, the
franchise athlete he was always meant to be.
A man never elected president. A man who must
now retire his fifty-two-beats-per-minute heartbeat
and live out a well-kept, well-protected, well-
manicured life, in the 100 percent high-energy
efficient Green House back on the ranch in
Crawford, Texas. On his way back to the GH
the Viking President, with his billions in bubbling
black gold, will fly past the lost city of New
Orleans, the rapidly melting North Pole, and
the hundreds of thousands dead in Iraq.

xvii

The hundreds of thousands dead of America,
the 1,836 ghosts of Katrina, mostly infants and
old folks, the failed domestic hunger and poverty
policies, the dead sons and dead daughters of the
long Volunteer State, each keen and curious IQ
of each and every child left behind, generations
of family farms, Dorothy's Kansas, and O-hi-o,
the protesting sorority of mothers who recently
reconvened, passing unanimous legislation to
never leave #43's dreams, to float in perpetuity,
with indefatigable, brass- and kryptonite-legged
sheep, marching and trudging, singing and bleat-
ing, refusing to go uncounted above the hills,
valleys, or golden arches of his Green House bed.

xviii

2011: Deep in Texas, his siesta ends. He climbs
out of the Green House bed, the ex-president
stoops over a pearl white sink and washes his hands
still wondering what "plunder" means. He decides
his smart Secretary of State was right. He should
have looked the word up before using it. At the
bottom of the GH stairs his librarian sweet-
heart is calling him for dinner. Outside, the GH
cistern is perfectly churning out the forty thousand
gallons needed to efficiently run the Green House.
At that moment a quiet divine rupture happens
far beneath the kelly green guard towers. It is a well-
oiled diamond cut breach. Even with the SS standing
guard at every station the GH water never saw it coming.

xix

We knew it was coming even if the clear rosewater of
Texas did not. The 1,836 ghosts of Katrina drilled &
fought their way through every protective oil well put
in their path and finally reached the other side of their
still devastated world. With his still perfect heartbeat
even more perfect than ever, the ex-president can still
easily take the stairs down to the dining room, laughing
all the way. At dinner he stands in order to propose
a toast to his old friend, the now retired prime minister,
who has come far across the great water to join him
for a quiet ex-state dinner. With Waterford hanging in
the air, soon to clink, the ex-president, with his perfect
heartbeat, makes his toast, "To the waters of Texas!
May they one day stop running so bloody red."

THE CONDOLEEZZA SUITE

Concerto no. 5: *Condoleezza & Intransigence*

At piano you are a major sound,
more than the articulate ivory key,
you hear things that aren't there.

On nightly TV, you open your mouth
to sing, a brilliant delayed count lifts,
subsides,

we take pride diving through
your Shostakovich gap. At news conferences,

you and they, cheek to cheek, are guillotined
& gutted, prepared, handled, neatly trussed
with jade and diamond thread.

You are the fifth little girl of Bombingham, found
recently, with ligature marks beneath high court

rulings, excavated with airbrush and Texas-size
picks, by not one, but two closely related

presidents, preserved forever in Washington
marble & the panning lights of CNN,

on display; the ruby carat curio, fresh,
from the roily rubble of integration.

Concerto no. 7: *Condoleezza {working out} at the Watergate*

Condoleezza rises at four,
stepping on the treadmill.

Her long fingers brace the two slim handles
of accommodating steel.

She steadies her sleepy legs for the long day ahead.
She doesn't get very far.

Her knees buckle wanting back
last night's dream.

[dream #9]

*She is fifteen and leaning forward from the bench,
playing Mozart's piano concerto in D minor, alone,
before the gawking, disbelieving, applauding crowd.*

not [dream #2]

*She is nine, and not in the church that explodes into dust,
the heart pine floor giving way beneath her friend Denise,
rocketing her up into the air like a jack-in-the-box
of a Black girl, wrapped in a Dixie cross.*

She ups the speed on the treadmill, remembering,
she has to be three times as good.

Don't mix up your dreams Condi.

She runs faster, back to the right, finally hitting her stride.
Mozart returns to her side.

She is fifteen again, all smiles, and relocated
to the peaks of the Rocky Mountains,

where she and the Steinway
are the only Black people in the room.

Concerto no. 11: *Condoleezza and the Chickering*

[In Italian, *con dolcezza* means "with sweetness"]

Angelena Rice, mother, second-generation piano master.
Music is deliberate, lush, summer-alive in the hot
Birmingham air. She is drawn to riff and scat, in the
tradition of the feet of fleeing slaves. Improvisation
darts like Ghanian goldfish in her blood.

Angelena Rice has chops.

> *She works all day.*
> *She can't teach the girl every little thing.*

Mattie Ray, grandmother, first-generation piano master,
the after-school-neighborhood-piano-teacher
of Black girls, on Dynamite Hill, of Condoleezza.

Mattie Ray knows her way to and from the woodshed,
but for Condoleezza, the stride piano is put away:

> *Practice. Practice. Practice.*
> *Steer your bright mind to Vulcan's torch—*
> *high atop Red Mountain.*
> *He alone will show you how to hammer*
> *out your notes into Roman thunder.*

When she is a girl she learns to play to the Italian
in her blood. She is third-generation Black girl with
sensual, graceful, doing fingers. No other Black girl
in Bombingham, with the sound of music emerald
set so deep in her heart, has ever been told over
Sunday dinner, while the gravy is still passing through
the air, *King is crazy.*

In the future, when she plays Secretary of State on the
world stage, the black keys will always be a stretch.

She will refuse to ever leave the Brahms-etched pages
that she has always counted on being open and before
her, Peter the Great, begging to commence.

When she is at her Watergate window, practicing
at her Chickering, she will, in the tradition of other
deposed heads, refuse to imagine grace notes &
half counts. She won't, not even when no one is
looking, sideslip or walk the white keys with only
the fingers of her left hand.

She will never ever close her eyes to a full spontaneous
pause nor understand the opium sweet of interlude
or diminished scale. The pleasure of imagining a
world outside of Mussorgsky's *Khovanshchina*
will elude her for the rest of her life. No one inside
her inner circle will suggest how else the dawning
new day might sound, if she would only—just this
once—take her eyes off the score.

Concerto no. 12: *Condoleezza Visits NYC {during hurricane season}*

The Ferragamos (finally) speak [out].

Like her husband, the president, her loyalty is legendary.
—ANONYMOUS BYSTANDER

That day we were just lazing around
on our sides, the TV was on
in the stockroom,
a typical hot afternoon camped out
in boats of big-city cardboard.

We heard the news that Big water had
broke loose, hit hard down South,
refused retreat. What we saw on the
flicker screen sat us up on our soles,
cross-toed, Mason Dixon style,
city heel arched, cracker barrel
eyes crossed, struck, staring.

From the deep cool folds of tissue paper
we could see the Buster Browns & Hush
Puppies, bloated & floating like loosed
animals, down that long new Mississippi.
Alongside high-top work boots and Kmart
house slippers there was debutante satin
and new bride peau de soie. My Lord—
the cross-mixing that was going on! Back
and forth we wondered what it must have
been like just to float away in the gushing
arms of the ultimate separation—Left shoe
stranded forever from her Right.

That water was one thousand heels high

(shoes most often
speak in the language of feet)

when Brother Sandal heard a commotion.
Stocky men with earplugs and wire, ugly
steel toes bumping down our aisles
in no time flat

(shoes most often
speak in the language of flats and heels).

They marched straight to the back of the store
knocking us off our stands and poking
their secret hands down our satiny private parts.
From high in the stacks we watched her shoeless
dillydally bringing up the rear. Oh! It was
her alright!

She was pretty gay about it all but didn't
come near divine, sequined me. I still got a
good look. I remember commenting, privately,
of course, to my Right, "Beautiful toes
for a secretary of state."

(The Right is never as empathetic
as the Left.)

Such a lovely arch—but after
two terms—not much support left.

The world always wants to see blood
gush from a turnip. But not me. No sir ree.

I knew from Inauguration #1
she was not the kind to trade places
(even in her mind) with anyone held hostage
on a roof by good old army corps levee water.
Her exquisite Saint John suits shouting into
the television screen: "Stranded bodies &
hard-headed water are not my department!"

One last thing. Right before leaving we heard
her ask the manager, on the down low:
"Do you sell ice skates
in my size?"

Imagine that, a woman of her perch
& position, inquiring about a blade.

The Head · over · Heels

Thunderbolt of Jove

> The width of the lightning bolt is only about as wide
> as a pencil.
>
> —THE WEATHER CHANNEL

The first saffron sheet breaks, two cumulous tin cans spill
a wide powder keg of gunpowder gray. Coiled thunder sparks
the inky nigrescent sky, rinds of one hundred oranges peel,
infuse, are slung. The mother goes flying. The daughter
takes to the glass.

Pots are topped. A stove shut down. The tiny kitchen stage
abandoned. The mother slips from flamingo to fleeing barn
owl. She spills: one widemouthed mason jar of liquid fear.
Her wild turning head is beak & breast pointed south,
toward the farther-further, darker, backside of the house.
She will only give herself to any windowless den, any
camouflage of cover: lavender snow quilt, moth-eaten
polka-dot coverlet, camphor woolens lost in the dark rib
of the closet, anything brother to lead, sister to opacity.

The only daughter stands at the sizzling window. As brown
moth, brazen & mesmerized, heedless, her nose wood-
peckered into the whirling world of the storm, thirsty
to call at the lightning, ambitious to burn, while the mother
throws her last warning out into the pitchfork of sky:

Lightning can come through any open
door, Girl. Can walk straight through
glass at any angle. Can take down
a little thing like you—just like that!

Out of view the mother freely dives. Prayer is the last light
spray of tongue-talk easing her safely down. Underneath

waves of mercerized cotton she will wait out the pageantry
of flashing orange light.

The girl is willing to be turned into the roar of rock, the float
of ash, just to feel its flashy fingers strike, to watch the fiery
sky pull at the tingling tips of her hands grazing the skin of
the glass. Her lips so close to self-suffocation, soon she is
choked back alive, the sky a fusillade of booms; air: florid,
tangerine jagged lines of corn-colored bombs.

At the weatherproof double panes her childhood lifts away
to the dusty locust field. Her fists, ripe with electricity, open
& close, her eyes are sweetly singed. The flutter-beat of her
lashes returns her to the softening sky, to the sight of her
self, on the other side of the kitchen glass, wet, staring back.

She begins shaking herself, back down from sky to earth.
Her stubborn lashes are two honey-drunk bumblebees still
tumbled on their backs. She has been fire-fed, rude. A girl
in levitation with the mad & thundering Jove. Going forward,
she is willing to go blind, lose her obeying-girl tongue, her
momentary sight, for any hot lemony tremble of the long
pencil's flash ever again.

The glass shows respect, staying warm for the mother's
return: She Stagolee-fumbles back into her kitchen. Sleepy
cotton stuck to her cheeks and hair. Her messy bonnet
needs to be retucked. But her eyes know a miracle
when they see one:

The girl is still there, still breathing, still camped out
at the unbroken glass, with a toothpick-size shadow
of resistance balanced in the flush of her lips. Done.

Nothing more to warn the girl against now. Now the long solemncholy wait, for the twisting out all the way. The final lift & turn, the wax and rock of childbirth evenly sculpted, the early pollinated melancholy, this sandy, burnished, smoldering lead of lanky Old Maid-to-be.

The Aureole
(for E)

I stop my hand midair.

If I touch her there everything about me will be true.
The New World discovered without pick or ax.

I will be what Brenda Jones was stoned for in 1969.
I saw it as a girl but didn't know I was taking in myself.

My hand remembers, treading the watery room,
just behind the rose-veiled eyes of memory.

Alone in the yard tucked beneath the hood of her car,
lucky clover all about her feet, green tea-sweet necklace
for her mud-pie crusty work boots.

She fends off their spit & words with silent two-handed
twists & turns of her socket wrench. A hurl of sticks &
stones and only me to whisper for her, from sidewalk far,

break my bones. A grown woman in grease-pocket overalls
inside her own sexy transmission despite the crowding of
hurled red hots. Beneath the hood of her candy-apple Camaro:

souped, shiny, low to the ground.

> The stars over the Atlantic are dangling
> salt crystals. The room at the Seashell Inn is
> $20 a night; special winter off-season rate.
> No one else here but us and the night clerk,
> five floors below, alone with his cherished
> stack of *Spiderman.* My lips are red snails
> in a primal search for every constellation

hiding in the sky of your body. My hand
waits for permission, for my life to agree
to be changed, forever. Can Captain Night
Clerk hear my fingers tambourining you
there on the moon? Won't he soon climb
the stairs and *bam!* on the hood of this car?
You are a woman with film reels for eyes.
Years of long talking have brought us to the
land of the body. Our skin is one endless
prayer bead of brown. If my hand ever lands,
I will fly past dreaming Australian Aborigines.
The old claw hammer and monkey wrench
that flew at Brenda Jones will fly across the
yard of ocean at me. A grease rag will be
thrust into my painter's pants against my
will. I will never be able to wash or peel
any of this away. Before the night is over
someone I do not know will want the keys
to my '55 silver Thunderbird. He will chase
me down the street. A gaggle of spooked
hens will fly up in my grandmother's yard,
never to lay another egg, just as I am jump-
ed, kneed, pulled finally to the high ground
of sweet clover.

Shaker: Wilma Rudolph Appears While Riding the Althea Gibson Highway Home

Fourteen months of mostly nights,
of pulling cheap depot blinds for privacy,
then the needle perfectly placed.

Coltrane's black and outstretched arm,
jumpy, my fingers jerk him to his dipping
feet, without warning, *A Love Supreme*

hemorrhages, midair. I make my walk
to the closet, undrunk but woozy, help
arrives from the slippery bleeding horn.

I am liquor-spinning in a fine dinner glass,
saxophone-tired from a week's worth of
work and no one to offer the door.

I pull out the Last Things, again: Lacy
frilly tops and bottoms that look nothing
like me, that more resemble her, clothes

never seen by her, things bought for
her unspoken leaving-eyes, things
hired to change her mind. *Why don't*

you stay? T-shirts. One whole year of silk
attempts, hope wrapped, unwrapped
rewrapped, in see-through paper, *Surprise!*

I dress up as the woman I could never be
in real life, then walk the runway before our
(former) bed, slowing, near the sailor's trunk,

at the church bench, one long curtsy near where
her soft owling mouth would always ease into
the headboard, a waterfall of hands, ghost clap.

Last night, the antique mirror finally caught me
from the heart down, this dual picture of myself:
the long-legged runner ghosting just above my

head, not one gray hair, but still recognizable by
the Girl Scout gap in my two front teeth. Runner
girl arched just under the broken-hearted woman.

The ghost calf taking in her milk while Guanyin
floats above them both, Zen guard of the firing
line, of every win or lose, rooted in the margin lane,

bowing to me and whispering to Wilma, *Don't dare
let her win.* Her sky-blue hat and thick black gun
pointing & ready to target when to burst. My long,

quivering, eight-hundred-yard relay legs, doing their
best not to give me away. One final bow of my head,
a blistering dig in of my soft girl heels, the interminable

wait for the finger of Guanyin to pull. The black gun,
the one-eyed stopwatch batting hard over my heart,
the girl chin ready, capable, bowed, for the high, red,

circuitous *try try again* of love. The watery track ink
black, shimmering, the dew, the unblemished air,
every love-light in the world lit, daring ahead, not behind,

everything at risk, to the left, to the right, now,
run baby—run.

Cattails

One woman drives across five states just to see her. The woman
being driven to has no idea anyone's headed her way. The driving
woman crosses three bridges & seven lakes just to get to her door.
She stops along the highway, wades into the soggy ground, cuts
down coral-eyed cattails, carries them to her car as if they might
be sherbet orange, long-stemmed, Confederate roses, sheared for
Sherman himself. For two days she drives toward the woman in
Kentucky, sleeping in rest areas with her seat lowered all the way
back, doors locked. When she reaches the state line it's misting.
The tired pedal-to-the-metal woman finally calls ahead. *I'm here,*
she says. *Who's this?* The woman being driven to, who has never
checked her oil, asks. The driving woman reminds her of the re-
cent writing workshop where they shared love for all things out-
of-doors and lyrical. *Come, have lunch with me,* the driving woman
invites. They eat spinach salads with different kinds of dressing.
They talk about driving, the third thing they both love and how
fast clouds can change from state line to state line. The didn't-
know-she-was-coming woman stares at she who has just arrived.
She tries to read the mighty spinach leaves in her bowl, privately
marveling at the driving woman's muscled spontaneity. She can
hardly believe this almost stranger has made it across five states
just to have lunch with her. She wonders where this mad driving
woman will sleep tonight. She is of two driving minds. One con-
vertible. One hardtop. The driving woman shows her pictures of
her children. Beautiful, the other does not say. Before long words
run out of petrol. The woman who is home, but without pictures
of her own, announces she must go. The driving woman frets &
flames, *May I walk you to your car?* They walk. The driver changes
two lanes in third gear, fast. The trunk opens. The Mario Andretti
look-alike fills the other woman's arms with sable-sheared cattails.

Five feet high & badly in need of sunlight & proudly stolen from across five states. The woman with no children of her own pulls their twenty pounds in close, resting them over her Peter-Panning heart. Her lungs empty out, then fill, then fill again with the surge of birth & surprise. For two years, until their velvet bodies begin (and end) to fall to pieces, every time the driven-to woman passes the bouquet of them, there, in the vase by the front door, she is reminded of what falling in love, without permission, smells like. Each time she reaches for her keys, she recalls what you must be willing to turn into for love: spiny oyster mushroom, damson, salt marsh, cedar, creosote, new bud of pomegranate, Aegean sage blue sea, fig, blueberry, marigold, leaf fall, frog's eye, dusty miller, thief-of-the-night.

Heirloom

Sundown, the day nearly eaten away,

the Boxcar Willies peep. Their
inside-eyes push black and plump

against walls of pumpkin skin. I step
into dying backyard light. Both hands

steal into the swollen summer air,
a blind reach into a blaze of acid,

ghost bloom of nacre & breast.
One Atlantan Cherokee Purple,

two piddling Radiator Charlies
are Lena-Horne lured into the fingers

of my right hand. *But I really do love you,*
enters my ear like a nest of yellow jackets,

well wedged beneath a two-by-four.

But I really didn't think I would (ever leave),
stings before the ladder hits the ground.

I swat the familiar buzz away.
My good arm arcs and aims.

My elbow cranks a high, hard cradle
and draws a fire. The end of the day's

sweaty air stirs fast in a bowl, the coming
shadows, the very diamond match I need.

One by one, each Blind Willie
takes his turn Pollocking the back

fence, heart pine explodes gold-leafed in
red and brown-eyed ochre. There is practice

for everything in this life. This is how
you throw something perfectly good away.

Orangerie

(for V)

> The way you make love is the way God will be with you.
>
> —RUMI

I

The arc of your boneless back flags above me.
We are blind discoverers, the nine seas pool
between us, blue curves, maritime, sheath of
surrender, limbed night.

What sweeter world could be voyaged from
the earth's center, pieced of figsuckle,
orange, the twice-licked skin of key limes,
breath of peppermint, braided, burning.

II

The long twin inches of my hands take the
whole night to ski the two pineapple halves
of you; brown baklava pieced over a caramel
cooler of skin. The monsoon is early.

Two marsupials coax deeper into the pouch of
wet night. Wandering inside the hour of the lung
hoping to turn conch by day. Our outside skins,
well brushed. Inside, we are desperate sandpaper,

breathless, the buttery lights of day sink into
dawn; two perfect halves of pink grapefruit,

skinned, twelve times crushed to velvet, lifted,
assumed to the inside flesh of new coconut.

A burning moon fossilizes, figs sway, right over
right, left dips left. *Don't fall,* is what you whisper,
back to you, in your sleep. It's too late to warn
the earth of the impression coming.

III

We wrap each other down, around, become
ground cover for every lonely night that ever was.

In the morning the monkeys come to eat what's
left of us. Talk is of the great storm, long gone
now. The older one, the Bishop, who never stops
filling his jaws & covering his eyes, listens back,

for one last thunder squall of fruit he hopes will
fall. He wants one last floating midnight-note to
drop like nine miles of ripe banana down the back
of his throat. He wants return, homily, consecration.

What was it that shook the blood oranges & bread-
fruit from our every tree? What left the roads
reduced, impassable?

What assuaged the purple hills all night, all the way
to the tea blue sea, cooling the fruit floating there,
twister of raw sugar, cubed, then row after row, ginger,
grated, peeled, dried, tangling tango of tongues.

The Clitoris

is 9 cm deep
in the pelvis.

Most of it scrunched & hidden.

New studies show
the shy curl
to be longer
than the penis,
but like Africa,
the continent,
it is never drawn
to size.

Mapmakers, and others, who draw
important things for a living,
do not want us to know this.

In some females,

> the clitoris stretches,
> unfurls,
> 8 in,
> with 2 to 3.5
> in, shaft free,
> outside the body.

> The longest clitoris of record
> has been found in the blue whale.

In water
desire can rise,
honor sea levels,
ignore land-locked
cartographers.

In water,
desire refuses retreat.

Brown Girl Levitation, 1962–1989

(for Beulah Lenorah Butler Davenport,
supreme watermelon, cantaloupe & pansy grower)

Something sharper than any blade cuts
the heavy roped balloon cord at the end
of my wrists; ascension begins. No tingle
of warning, just the thin, rising held-breath
of a brown girl, super sudden lift, then,
the instinctive dive & grab for anything
dependable, two ton, well tethered, close:

Shaggy, heavy-bellied, near blind sheep dog.
Bulbous, well-rooted, yellow meat watermelon.
Iron held, black leather, Detroit-Buick car arm.
Steel blue, cavernous, baby brother crib roof.
Brass, honeycomb canopy, octopus jungle gym.
Mesozoic era, roots, trunk, cane field of azalea.

I could smell it inching closer to full power,
like a storm nearing from across the field of
my young life. Except, it wasn't over there,
coming. It was inside, gaining on me, blooming.
I could not grab my girl hat and run. Could not
turn my long yellow feet into brown girl spikes
and beat it home. Wherever I happened to be
when it hit—I had to hunker down.

I would lean hard into that high, elephant-lifting wind
with everything I had, carrying my girl mind & muscle
to the thing that I knew had been grandmother sent,
engineered, just for me. And there she would appear:

straw hat, cotton dress, cow boots, rabbit grass stogie
between her two front teeth, walking the dirt road back
to the old homehouse. Her humming heart in mighty step
with the bee wings of the July air. Her arms full of as many
bowling-ball headed, green-striped melons as she could manage.
The red sweet flesh, the jet-eyes, my just-in-time juicy
body weights passed from her arms to my lap,
until the great gray wind retreated & agreed
that I'd had enough & turned
me loose, disappearing back
beyond, into the indigo
heaven, until the next
lifting time.

The Head · Waters

Dancing with Strom

I want to tell you, ladies and gentlemen, there's not enough
troops in the army to force the southern people to break
down segregation and accept the Negro [pronounced Nigra]
into our theatres, into our swimming pools, into our homes,
and into our churches.

—STROM THURMOND, SOUTH CAROLINA
SENATOR AND PRESIDENTIAL CANDIDATE
FOR THE STATES' RIGHTS PARTY, 1948

I said, "I'm gonna fight Thurmond from the mountain to
the sea."

—MODJESKA MONTEITH SIMKINS, CIVIL
RIGHTS MATRIARCH, SOUTH CAROLINA, 1948

The youngest has been married off.

He is as tall as Abraham Lincoln. Here, on his
wedding day, he flaunts the high spinning laugh
of a newly freed slave. I stand above him, just
off the second-floor landing, watching
the celebration unfold.

Uncle-cousins, bosom buddies, convertible cars
of nosy paramours, strolling churlish penny-
pinchers pour onto the mansion estate. Below,
Strom Thurmond is dancing with my mother.

The favorite son of South Carolina has already
danced with the giddy bride and the giddy bride's
mother. More women await: Easter dressy,
drenched in caramel, double exposed, triple cinched,
lined up, leggy, ready.

I refuse to leave the porch.

If I walk down I imagine he will extend his
hand, assume I am next in his *happy darky* line,
#427 on his dance card. His history
and mine, burnt cork and blackboard chalk,
concentric, pancaked, one face, two histories,
slow dragging, doing *the nasty.*

My father knows all this.

Daddy's Black Chief Justice legs straddle the boilerplate
carapace of the CSS *H. L. Hunley,* lost Confederate
submarine, soon to be found just off the coast of
Charleston. He keeps it fully submerged by
applying the weight of every treatise he has
ever written against the death penalty of
South Carolina. Chanting "Briggs v. Elliott,"
he keeps the ironside door of the submarine shut.
No hands.

His eyes are a Black father's beacon, search-
lights blazing for the married-off sons, and
on the unmarried, whale-eyed, nose-in-book
daughter, born unmoored, quiet, yellow,
strategically placed under hospital lights to
fully bake. The one with the most to lose.

There will be no trouble. Still, he chain-
smokes. A burning stick of mint & Indian
leaf seesaws between his lips. He wants
me to remember that trouble is a fire that
runs like a staircase up then down. Even
on a beautiful day in June.

I remember the new research just out:

What the Negro gave America
Chapter 9,206:

Enslaved Africans gifted porches to North
America. Once off the boats they were told,
then made, to build themselves a place—to live.

They build the house that will keep them alive.

Rather than be the bloody human floret on
yet another southern tree, they imagine higher
ground. They build landings with floor enough
to see the trouble coming. Their arced imaginations
nail the necessary out into the floral air. On the
backs and fronts of twentypenny houses,
a watching place is made for the ones who will
come tipping with torch & hog tie through the
quiet woods, hoping to hang them as decoration
in the porcupine hair of longleaf.

The architecture of Black people is sui generis.
This is architecture dreamed by the enslaved:

Their design will be stolen.
Their wits will outlast gold.
My eyes seek historical rest from the kiss-
kiss theater below; Strom Thurmond's
it's-never-too-late-to-forgive-me *chivaree.*
I search the tops of yellow pine while my
fingers reach, catch, pinch my father's
determined-to-rise smoke.

Long before AC African people did the
math: how to cool down the hot air of
South Carolina?

If I could descend, without being trotted
out by some roughrider driven by his
submarine dreams, this is what I'd take
my time and scribble into the three-tiered,
white crème wedding cake:

Filibuster. States' Rights. The Grand Inquisition
of the great Thurgood Marshall. This wedding
reception would not have been possible without
the Civil Rights Act of 1957 (opposed by
you-know-who).

The Dixiecrat senator has not worn his
sandy seersucker fedora to the vows.
The top of Strom Thurmond's bald head
reveals a birthmark tattooed in *contrapposto*
pose: *Segregation Forever.*

All my life he has been the face of hatred;
the blue eyes of the Confederate flag,
the pasty bald of white men pulling wooly
heads up into the dark skirts of trees,
the sharp, slobbering, amber teeth of
German shepherds, still clenched inside
the tissue-thin, (still-marching), band-leader
legs of Black schoolteachers, the single-
minded pupae growing between the legs of
white boys crossing the tracks, ready to
force Black girls into fifth-grade positions,
Palmetto state-sanctioned sex 101.

I don't want to dance with him.

My young cousin arrives at my elbow.
Her beautiful lips the color of soft-skin
mangoes. She pulls, teasing the stitches

of my satin bridesmaid gown, "You better
go on down there and dance with Strom—
while he still has something left."

I don't tell her it is unsouthern for her
to call him by his first name, as if they
are familiar. I don't tell her: To bear
witness to marriage is to believe that
everything moving through the sweet
wedding air can be confidently, *left*—
to Love.

I stand on the landing high above the
beginnings of Love, holding a plastic
champagne flute, drinking in the warm
June air of South Carolina. I hear my
youngest brother's top hat joy. Looking
down I find him, deep in the giddy crowd,
modern, integrated, interpretive.

For ten seconds I consider dancing with
Strom. His Confederate hands touch
every shoulder, finger, back that I love.
I listen to the sound of Black laughter
shimmying. All worry floats beyond
the gurgling submarine bubbles,
the white railing, every drop of
champagne air.

I close my eyes and Uncle Freddie
appears out of a baby's breath of fog.
(The dead are never porch bound.)
He moves with ease where I cannot.
He walks out on the rice-thrown air,

heaving a lightning bolt instead of
a wave. Suddenly, there is a table set,
complete with 1963 dining room stars,
they twinkle twinkle up & behind him.
Thelonious, Martin, Malcolm, Nina,
Dakota, all mouths Negro wide &
open have come to sing me down.
His tattered almanac sleeps curled like
a wintering slug in his back pocket.
His dark Dogon eyes jet to the scene
below, then zoom past me until they are
lost in the waning sugilite sky. Turning
in the shadows of the wheat fields,
he whispers a truth plucked from
the foreword tucked in his back pocket:
Veritas: Black people will forgive you
quicker than you can say *Orangeburg
Massacre.*

History does not keep books on the
handiwork of slaves. But the enslaved
who built this Big House, long before
I arrived for this big wedding, knew
the power of a porch.

This native necessity of nailing down
a place, for the cooling off of air,
in order to lift the friendly, the kindly,
the so politely, the in-love-ly, jubilant,
into the arms of the grand peculiar,
for the greater good of
the public spectacular:

us
giving us
away.

Segregation, Forever

(Three Black boys {strike oil} in the street [after the rain]:
a comic strip.)

> There was a time when the shallow warm seas were
> filled with coral, starfish, and flower-like echinoderms,
> some were free swimming, but most were fixed by a stem,
> surrounded, by a circlet of arms.
> —*FOSSILS: A GUIDE TO PREHISTORIC LIFE*

Three {Black boys} hurl like invertebrates
to reach the top of the earth wall first. They:

loose sea lilies cut on their hinge line,
above thorax, below septum. They,

fly-float with the help of quick feet,
skating to peer a new precipice. Hoisted &

held by their own giggles. They:
counterpoint and twain, three Picassos,

without the matador's interfering prick
or keening European brush. Oshun's

fingers, six million years long, suspend
each of their high notes. Three {Black boy}

bodies dervish and dangle, their ancient
sound fills every sidewalk crack in the

new world. A Benin pointer aligns, then
slingshots their heads and lips, while Kuba

thumbs drill then spread wide their toes,
the street Spidermans beneath them. Where

they twist and shout pyramids stretch
into one sheet of long black water. Carpets

of {Black boy} joy spill all the way down. Six plum-
paneled perfect arms stretch, into six waving sails,

their open mouths, Simone-esque. A red
Jemima-joy rows them all the way to the end.

They play on the eleven thousandth runway
named for Martin Luther King, Jr.

On approach they curve away
like Onychaster, brittle beloved

animal flora, from the Mississippian.
I aperture into prickly, 345-million-year-old

net. They are the last great mammals to appear,
before the last great rain. So far,

how we got here, why we stayed, no brownie box
jubilation of historical life is ever lost on their feet.

My arms twist into barbed 1940s chicken wire,
the twenty-six lion-mouth alphabets of Ida B. Wells rise,

into bale and bill {of sale}, all along
my abdomen I roll out the patent pending

numbers of Black inventors. They dangle
like eastern star mason pendants in between

their wild fragrant street dance, then fall away
like New Orleans' Mardi Gras beads;

the *l*'s, the *e*'s, even the *p*'s, chain link, then
spill behind their Watusi-wide, Daddy Grace slide.

All three, together, remind me of the black rapids
of 1919, Tennessee Valley, no warning,

just a freakish summer Sunday breach of river
laying everything down, bringing

everything up. From here I know their rocketing
joy must go unrecognized. The Good News of their

pure monkeyshine chicanery must be put away now.
All headlines and any waiting new world phylum

must never be reported or filed. Their Black boy joy,
on this slick well-named street, must remain untelevised.

I know history &
(you know) what happens next.

Negroes with Guns

If I'm a criminal for advocating that people have the right to
defend themselves and fight for what they deserve, then
I hope I'm always known as a criminal.

—ROBERT F. WILLIAMS, PRESIDENT OF NAACP,

MONROE, NORTH CAROLINA, 1954

The father pulls the six-paneled heart pine door
open, leading her out by the arm, first lesson.
They wind behind the house, past the prayer trees.

Beyond the woods, back back of the shed,
into the hush hush air
where prayer and camp meeting
rose like jasmine vine,
back in the black code days.

Their walk together, through the fall sun, into
the old old woods, has been written by carpenter
pencil on the wide-block insurance calendar
for fifteen years,

since the day Miss Longfellow, hinterland
midwife, left behind one extralong, glistening
brown taffy baby, rolled, safe & center
of the white white sheet.

The escort-father moves easy through the
loblolly, one hand on his Smith & Wesson
(his apple-eyed German luger sleeps like
a cub in his waistband)
one hand gentling her shooting arm,
never pulling. Her head, hawk high;

her eyes, bog-turtle low;
her breath full of
one last useless resist:

Why I have to do what she do?

At the speckled breathy chicken wire door
stands the one afraid of heights, who can
blow the *x* out the Maxwell House can
can, who knows that nothing that comes
in twos, on her, was ever taught to squint.

The mother-markswoman, dressed in
cotton smock & brogans, stares at
the leaving leaving backsides of the two
she would jump out of any aeroplane for.
When she practices shooting the eyes out
of a carpet beetle, her toes tend to rise rise,
but she cannot swim, fly, leave land,
with ease.

Years later strangers will arrive at her door
and try try to interview her for their
Black People Who Refused to Join King
documentary. She will announce at the same
breathy chicken wire of a door to the black
black eye of the camera: ,

What goes on in the backwoods
stays on in the backwoods.

Turning back to her pots with nary a sound,
her trigger finger slick & wet, wrinkled,
soapy, content for now, devoted for now
to coaxing egg & cheese off a casserole dish.

For now she stops her kitchen work but
not her kitchen worry worry. She hears
the first pulse of thunder break. Her ears
stretch & preen the bright sure sun and
half mile of trees, the field. She closes her
eyes hoping to see where her two honey
buns are going even before their feet reach
the fault lines   there.

Her brown hands, covered in twice-sifted
paprika & goose flour, twitch. The morning
has her mindless & stuttering, forgetting
her hurricane of work ahead. She touches
the itch near her nose. A speckle of whitish
wheat will dot her face there. Her husband,
the noticer, his hands not even off the copper
knob, will reach, sweetly, for her dark dark
gingerbread of face, poppy of white.

She will never realize this errant bloom of
white was ever there. She will only care
that he returned to her, found something
out of place (on her) and fixed it. Just like
the time time before and the time time ahead.

How she do?
She'll ask.

Fruit don't run from where it falls.
He'll answer.

Back in the kitchen her hands rest on the
red cake bowl where the fatty chicken thighs,
her daughter's favorite, bob & dive, dive &
bob, like synchronized swimmers, all-you-
can-eat, the Berlin Olympics, 1936. Jesse

had already won. Adolph commenced biting
at the skin of his pearl white fists. Tanned with
fresh garlic, the thighs bubble up and practice
sleep, inside the silky clabber of milk butter
stretching into a colored Swan Lake. Greens,
settled and woozy woozy, collapse inside
a steaming bog of pot liquor.

At the knotty rusty screen, the mother who
can shoot the first and second *s* from out
the middle of grasshopper, without browning
the grass or decapitating the hop hop, stares
out into the field of yellowing pine for sign
of insect life or other other.

The trees unwrap. Gunpowder lifts every leaf
into air, cabbage-colored cicadas *lickety-split:*
Lucky life released. Her wide toes widen on the
wooden threshold, shaved three times, with his
three different-sized scythes, over three winding
weeks. Her steel wool heels bear down down on
the well-buttered heart pine taking the wood in
like cornbread poured out on a hot griddle,

just behind her
the pig iron smokes.

Hash Marks

Drayton Hall Plantation

(for South Carolina and Its Corridor of Shame)

The blue bonnet children had a wall.
The swimming swamp dogs too.

Their hash marks of height play
peek with the same canary sun.

Plantation measurements of progress:

See this is them on two legs,
this higher one here—on four.

On this tour, every visitor, but one, gets misty-
eyed concerning the preservation of the pencil lines.

Where is the wall that brims the height & progress
of the Nigras?

Sheetrock record of crosscut backs,
split hymens, slit bellies, sold-away sons.

No recordings from the precise recorders of these,
to honey other calculations that grandfather time.

What is here for me in the Big House is suspended,
afloat in bee amber. Each long drawn, lost longing,

root cellared, pickled, airtight, dunked
in blue glass jars, wax-dripped tops, shout
& twist.

Men Who Give Milk I

> Breast development occurs commonly, and spontaneous
> lactation occasionally, in men under conditions of starvation.
> —*DISCOVER* MAGAZINE, FEBRUARY 1995

In Toronto, there is a man with Wole Soyinka hair,
walking one way, a giant garbage bag bobbles in his arms;

now and then, he looks another way,
behind, where another bag sits.
He does not turn for it, not then,
instead he pays attention to his future,
walking all the way ahead.

Down the street he goes tipping,
a tightrope walker's agility. His bag,
as bulbous as a giant's eye,
cannot help him see.

People with steaming cups & toasted
breads push to not be in his way. His whole
wide world is on the move.

I keep one eye on him and his moving
bag. The other eye is kept on the bag
of his corner-past.

He reaches the end of the street, sits the bag
in his arms down on the corner, gentles it,
as if it is a sack of the last time he heard the
high yellow & coral orange of his mother's
laugh, before, when his world had a lock,
a key, a ceiling, floor, a proper place for her
to cup his lion-eyed face.

As he leaves he pats the bag on its belly, U-turns,
walks two blocks back to the other bag, squats,
picks that bag up, turns forward, again, once again,
walking, walking.

His walk is strong, as if he has children, three,
one wife to love until the end, a thirty-year mortgage,
a niggling boss;
Keep your shiny quarters!
his feet sing out to the bread pushers.

He does not stop at the first corner, or the second corner
with his first bag. He walks beyond, into his future,
to the third corner, where he sits the bag in his arms,
the bag of his dreams, down.

He settles his hand on this bag's spine, as if
it is that day in the country with his father—
when it was about to rain,

> *This is how to shift & glide,* the old man says.
> The old four-speed truck lurches like a bullfrog.
> Two hours of repeat instruction and the old man
> finally reaches for the boy's temple, his hand,
> an onyx butterfly landing on a purple bush it both
> fears and fancies. (This is the first time his father
> has ever touched him.) The boy's able parking
> between two old oaks, laying down the sure
> smooth tracks of the man-to-be.

The walking man, with hair like Wole Soyinka,
stands & turns away from this noonday flash
of the ephemeral.

He goes back for the sunshine bag that is fat with his
laughing mother who is always reaching, even now,

for his browning & walking face. He walks it to the corner
beyond the bag spilling with his finally satisfied father,
and his satisfied father's finally soaring butterflies.

This picking up and putting down, this serpentine
stepping goes on until the sun gives up, raises its
red-orange hand, going to work in some other
hemisphere.

All day, all week, the pendant, then crescent, then
waning whole winter moon pours. With every step
his feet stitch, then unbraid, the wooly strings of his
heart keep moving.

His two bags never meet on the same corner.
Every thing now out of his reach is never out of
his arms—for long.

In Toronto, a man zigzags his way across Canada.
In Canada, a Black man stitches himself to earth.

Alice Butler

(for James T. Hill, Uncle Junior*)*

We stand shoulder to waist in her backyard.
I am leaving. Something, my grandmother says,
I do *very well.*

We have come from burying her favorite sister.
Beulah Davenport has outlived them all. A white
dove resembling a lost bird off a soapbox

lands on the mean neighbor's roof
two hundred feet away. We rarely look that way
unless we have to. We have to.

The white bird, we both know, has never
set foot in the air of South Carolina before.
We know this without saying a word into that air.

Never have we seen so white a bird before. In the
middle of remembering the white and yellow flowers
of the service, the white bird has landed, smack-dab

in the middle of our sad-joy. *She looked real good,*
grandmother had just pronounced. Right then
the whiter-than-white bird, which had never before

set wing or beak in the air of South Carolina, began
his march down the cold lip of the mean neighbor's
tin roof, landing finally on the speckled rim of the

washtub. Now, the whiter-than-white bird is as close
as a kiss we both want to know. All sweet funerary
talk has stopped. My grandmother is ninety-five. Nothing

on her trembles. But this, the whitest bird in the world,
prancing about on a tin tub in South Carolina, does.
In a voice borrowed from a diamond miner, carefully,

she taps, breaking the air into baby blue shards,
Alice, Sister, that you? I do not move, comfort, or join in
this moment in any way. All around us, lavishly private.

More private than a modest woman lifting her dress
to a lover, for the first time. More delicate than the
lace around this old woman's favorite sitting chair,

in the front room
of the white clapboard house,
leaning just behind us.

For three days, the granddaughter, who by then has
lived up to what she is best known for, is her usual
four hundred miles away, when she gets her three o'clock

call. The pearl-white-bird report comes in like regular,
RCA Victor news, spoken from the crackling wired fabric
of voice box & ears. On the fourth day the call arrives

a little later. The diamond miner's voice has dug down,
a few feet deeper. I am the oldest granddaughter. It is
a report given for only me to hear:

She's all the way across now, Child. Just wanted to let
me know she made it free & clear. "Beulah," she told me,
"when you get here, remember, heaven will only
let you out to pass back good news."

Penguin, Mullet, Bread

She pulls white oily meat of mullet
off the long sharp bones of spine.
The bones prick. She never once
says, *Ouch!* kissing the tips, now
and then. I watch her long fingers.
Seven inches away, my eyes are two glossy olives glued

to the delicate woman's mouth.
It is summer, behind her, the white
curtains she has made move like
sea grass, tall, freckled, waving just
beyond. I am camera. She is movie.
She bites, then rolls, placing plump soft chunks of fish

into the side of her mouth. Her eyes
grow big from what she tastes.
I study her mouth not her eyes.
Watching her eyes is for later, night-
time, when she will read the day's
story to me. She chews slowly, never showing what's there.

Her tongue twists and falls. My dinner
moves in slow whitefish animation.
She coos like a woman who can taste
any flavor in the world. A woman
who can hula-hoop in her own mouth.
My hand rises. My fingers reach, fall short, then fall, again.

I want to say: *Mama, pull the flesh
from the throat not the belly.* The meat
there has more juice than the meat
around the fins. But she is the mama.

I have no baby patois for what little
I know of watery things. I have only seventeen months of new

desire, and only two ways of showing
it. It's too soon to tell her how much
I miss my private swimming hole,
that, by the size six looks of her, has
all but dried up. That story must
wait for nine birthday candles, when I am headlong back

in her warm water. She chews down
on the flesh of the fish, packs it around
good until it is a perfect caramel mush.
Catching some of the juice that falls
with her longest finger, there at the
corner of her mouth, she pushes all of the sweet flesh back inside.

Once or twice, she pulls out a hatpin-
size bone hiding in the waves of tender
meat. Only then does she wear her
Eureka smile. Holding it up in the air
to show. My wishful eyes rise. Her long
hand is circled in light. My body shifts into question mark, grateful.

My newish eyes lift over & beyond
the white curtains that all visitors
believe are store bought. *This is why
you have a mama,* her empire backbone
finally speaks. *Why you must never talk
back. Why you must love, honor, obey. My job,* her toes pas de deux,

*is to feed and tell you the stories, & keep
you away from sharp things that might
slip into your throat and never completely
disappear.* Her eyes plié into the slinky

circles of her mouth. The sweet flesh
is finally ground. Salt & snapper, spit & meal, are a fine pâté.

She reaches her long brown fingers
deep inside her jaw. Our hinged mouths
open, mine prematurely. My fists are
flying fleshy verbs in the apple air of
her kitchen, balled in sweet anticipation.
Chubby legs yoga-extend into early orgasmic pose, my chin sets,

downward facing dog. My begging eyes
& dark mauve lips close in slow around
her fingers. The pounded succulent
fish & spit lands center of my tongue.
I swell in my first chair ever. Fed by
the mother who relishes the story of turning her back & leaving me,

once, to swim off a thousand miles,
find food,
fight off shimmering shark,
then swim a thousand miles back,
just to drop her beak into mine.

I am the lucky girl of the high chair.

Liberty Street Seafood

I stand in line. Behind me the hungry stretch & wiggle
out the door. Sterling cake bowls nestle in ice:

mullet   striped bass   whiskered cat   rock shrimp
steel porgies   blue crab   "No eel 'til Christmas"

mother mussels   flat-face flounder   sleeping snapper
whiting   one sea turtle   (lazy fisherman).

In his fishmonger-owner apron Randy is white, round
as a blowfish, conducting this orchestra of desire.

Members: the cut boys and the lined up, who come
every day and wait in between frozen ice and hot oil.

The cut boys are well suited in fish scale and high up
on risers above us. They sing out with their knives.

Stationed inside tiny cutting booths slashing this throat
and that. Fish tune.

Veritas: Those who are exquisite at beheading
always occupy a throne.

One has a giant Afro. Another's hair is finely braided
backward, like flattened rows of corn. The half-straight

ends of his thick black wool curl up his neck like one large
fin. The last one has shaved and greased his head for duty.

Old men who sit around, outside the front door, tease.
Early on they named him, *Dolphin.* He is playful, jumpy,

slick, far more endangered than the other two. All three
wear the heavy rubber smocks of men who use their

hands to kill (& feed). All three hold knives longer than their
johnsons. For now, they are safe. The wet wood engulfs

them from the waist down. Cleaned fish: their handiwork
will soon be on display at ninety-six dinner tables, Southside.

We pass the time by lying:

How you do?
Fine.

Alabaster fish scales streak & dot their hair like Mardi
Gras keepsakes. Fish petals float into the wet air.

Black. Indian. Zulu. Sequined, smelly, bloody scales settle
across three sets of brown hands, arms, in muscle shirts.

Scales thick as white evening gloves. The cut boys turn
each fish over like one-eyed fabric dolls. One has his

Mama Helene's eyelashes. He is the jittery dolphin
on the loose. A hand-me-down Afro pick sits in No. 2's

back pocket. This one with a tail always on his neck
has a fist always on his comb, circa 1975, belonging

to his brother, thrown under the jail, up under in upstate
Connecticut. Cause: a bad fight about a *chica* gone jugular.

These cut boys, shine jewel & scale, stationed before a wall
of black & silver ways & means. Eastern Star daughters and

North Star slaves stare out at the hungry through their
notched eyes. They whisper and laugh, loving how we wait

on them. Three Black boys in hip hop haute couture, in suits
of bloody, rubber smocks, standing side by side, making

three dollars an hour, beheading and detailing fish.
Their long knives whacking pine all day. Fish eyes roll.

So Friday is made. The white man reaches
for the money, faces the hungry,

his back fully turned,
their knives just above his head.

Head Off & Split

If I could go back, I'd run.

—GEORGE C. JONES

the car rolls down the driveway   Christmas is as far away
as it ever was   only the only daughter leaving   remains
north to south   smoke rises   the two that she is perfect
opposite halves of are on fire   three heads burn

fire tumbles out of the father's hand   leaps the alley
jumps next to the mother   one more thing the daughter
cannot control   or put out   before leaving the car
inches off   the mother   flames head to toe   mother

takes off running   first   into the garage   then inside
the ranch style house   she is the more able   the more
dramatically inclined   holding the five mph wheel
the daughter follows the script   salty eyes close &

trace   the mother's feet move inside the house   mother
moves in an all-out sprint   the daughter knows when
where exactly she will turn   arms ghost dance with
every sharp turn in the room   a warm breeze enters

the car   as the mother's arm sees another sleeve   wearing
eyes and fur   in front of the grandfather clock   she stops
reaches   into the open closet   slips on the hand-me-down
Dorothy Dandridge mink coat   turning the front knob

the mother swings the door wide   she runs the seven
steps of porch   smiling   unspent   as if there has been
a treasure found   something in her hand   remembered for
the leaving daughter   has almost been forgotten   she makes

it to the front of the house   where the car and the daughter
that were leaving now idle   the father smokes   wondering
if the rain will come   as promised   it always rains when his
Lovechild leaves   should he cut the city water on   or give

the clouding day a chance   the sight of the mother   standing
in something else's skin   makes the daughter   roll down
the glass between them   one last time   she reaches out her
arm   their palms touch   they have the same vein-rich hands

just different colors   a cooler of water gathers in the mother's
eyes   this mother and father   are not front-yard cast-iron
figurines   not jockeys   there are no hay forks   they are
Catlett's cut in soapstone   Black and striking   on parent stilts

in front of the house   where the girl was raised   be strong
love capable   taught right from rich   the rich can be poor
the architect Black   the builder   of every house in view   Black
and bare-handed   pencil behind his ear   she has seen these

two stand this way   near the curb of this house   for fifty years
she has left them here on this curb   803 times   counting
today   she wonders   what else has been left here   on this curb
for the rainwater   to hold tight   to wash down   into the

drinking water   the full-length mink hides   the pajamas of
the mother   everyone gathered for the morning goodbye
smells   of fried fish and grits   sacred Sunday morning goodbye
food   made especially for only daughters   who have perfected

the art of leaving   water can be seen   in every eyelet of mother
percale   his seersucker   the head of the mink stirs   no longer
wanting to see the world   through the taxidermist's hands
there is the usual five-alarm   longing   the wet-eyed mother

puts one hand in her pocket   cups   the other   to her mouth
Steam the drapes before you hang them, Dear   new drapes
made for the daughter's first house   roll about in the trunk
velvet swaddled newborns   in a mother's well-kept attic plastic

the car picks up speed   glue poured on the road   earlier in
the day   by the father   slows her   when he first rose to check
the height of the grass from the day before   three throats
thicken   *Remember, anything worth doing is worth doing well.*

the daughter   closes her cloudy eyes around the mother's
mink words   there is a skin between them   stretching   made
of wax and iron   the flames leap at the bumper as it moves
away   the mother wants to be happy   she has a daughter

who can drive herself   up and down the road   the mother's
eyes have turned into an ocean   mourning waves   leave
for the open shore again   the dark wide open sea for both
is just ahead   she covers her face with her beautiful dark hands

the diamonds that he gave her over the years   dazzle   Sunday
morning sun is refracted   on every straw of pine   she never
takes them off   not even to cook the canned salmon   that she
raised her family on   the father   leaning on the mailbox

is resigned to his life   without his Lovechild   without any
daughters of his only daughter   climbing up his arms   his wife
curves   into her handed-down mink   the animal refuses
to open its eyes   pulling the snarling head up around her ears

she sinks into its growling sharp-toothed mouth with the news
the not news   there will be no grandchildren   the coat has
no one   to be handed down to   the only daughter is down
the drive   already staring   into the rearview   waving   salmon &

grits her perfume   the mama   even without makeup   is still
the most beautiful woman in the world   the daughter   is leaving
again   she waves again   just as the flames reach   the perimeter
the burning father's lips   the wild mark of fire is left in the yard

is that rain

ii

as the two get smaller in the rearview   the fishmonger
steps close   right where the corner meets the highway
the Robert Johnson turn   here   the fishmonger always
steps out to greet her leaving   wearing his smock-robe

of holiday white   Thanksgiving   Christmas   Easter
he is the crossing guard   of her goodbye   before turning
onto the big highway   she must   pass through his knives
his sharp high-held blade   waving there at the ready

her neck   pulled taut   pushed back   into the headrest
as far back   as a daughter's neck will go   her eyes shut
no need to look behind   any longer   he will not need
his usual two whacks today   his one whale knife

with sixteen braids   of carbon steel   will do   the handle
ergonomically swank   she hands her long neck over
the fishmonger's blade falls quick   the mother & the mink
have made up   the father's rain-soaked hand touches lips

iii

My disconnected eyes glaze over   I have a long way
to drive without my head   The thinking part of me
wobbles   Then falls   The exquisite tip of his knife
enters at the lip of my sternum   Then dives   Down

to the Cheerio of my navel   The blade licks then
stops   The protective limestone beds are of no use
My A+ blood spills   On the leather cutting board
my throat separates from the rest of me   I am fully

awake   Once again   The eggnog anesthesia from the
long holiday visit has not worked   I am aware of all
the pulling   The tugging   All the hands on the inside
of me   Doing their business   Making a Daytona

500 of my lungs   I am unable to do anything about it
Those who are suited up don't know   I am awake
In every *New England Journal* this is called unethical
The fishmonger lays me on the table   He chooses a

smaller knife for the rest of my drive   The skin of my
torso is peeled back to reveal   What is left   What it will
take for me to leave them behind   The 803rd time
How can I drive back to my life ahead   Each time the

leaving hardens the soft tissue of my birth   This time
he says   He will only take the head and the pearl green
eyes   Next time he says   The lungs   The heart sac
The liver   Will all have to go along   What can you do

in this life without the parts you need   To feel the bend
in the road?   I am head off & split   Perfectly served
The daughter   Home as expected   Without children
of her own   As unexpected   No little hands & legs to beg

To run the dusty dirt road giggling   As the wagon turns
toward the homehouse   The waving mother knows
there will be no one to follow   The leaving daughter has
outgrown home   She must drive out to the beyond alone

In the haze of the fishmonger's operation   A delicate clamor
Sharp instruments are picked up then laid down   I hear the
others in the next room bidding   Auctioning for my lady parts
Since I won't use them   The fishmonger begins to whistle

The hard specialized work is done   They hand him their tiny
numbered papers   They pay well for the parts of me   I won't
use   He puts me on ice   Saving my lady parts in sections
The savory pieces will be bought quickly   Futures are offered

The lights   The liver   Go first   Holidays come in pairs
Time for sauce & condiment   Pâté   Jams   Jellies   All
needed for the fertile feast of me   He reaches for the roll of
waxy white paper   To dress me   There is a line of others

There will never be enough of me to go around
A woman in yacht and sailing attire with too much
makeup   Has her hand outstretched   We resemble
by way of our un-stretched marks   I do not wish to

go home with her   But I am head off & split   It's no
longer my call   The celebration has already begun
The fishmonger is busier today than usual   He can
get more for me by dicing more of me   The cash

register is nearly musical   He usually pays such good
attention   To what he is selling   To whom he sells
His attentiveness   Keeps me returning to him
Time after time   I lay my head back to make my

final turn onto the highway   He is the one who runs
his finger down my seams   To be sure I am clean
The pink flesh of my insides await   Always   I am
spongy to his touch   I never complain   But here at

the end   Today   He has not taken his time with me
He has not noticed   My giggling pouch of new fat
Up under my lady parts   The long orange sac of bubbly
roe lumbering for attention   Down in the aging galley

of me   Quivering between my tiny sharp dorsal fins
Beneath my primary spout   This part of me that each
and every time is conveniently ignored is full today
Surprise!   He does not hesitate   The coral bed of my

afterlife is washed into the drain   Without comment
The highest bidder raises her hand   I am tossed into
the icy silver bowl   A lifetime of waiting   Hungering
to be called   Delicious

Absolutely unmixed attention is prayer.

—SIMONE WEIL

Instruction, Final: To Brown Poets from Black Girl with Silver Leica

Be camera, black-eyed aperture. Be diamondback terrapin, the only animal that can outrun a hurricane. Be 250 million years old. Be isosceles. Sirius. Rhapsody. Hogon. Dogon. Hubble. Stay hot. Create a pleasure that can stir up the world. Study the moon with a pencil. Drink the ephemerides. Lay with the almanacs. Become the lunations. Look up the word *southing* before you use it in a sentence. Know *southing* is not a verb. Imitate them remarkable days. Locate all your ascending nodes. Chew eight times before you swallow the lyrics and silver lamentations of James Brown, Abbey Lincoln, Al Green, Curtis Mayfield, and Aretha. Hey! Watch your language! Two and a Quarter is not the same as Deuce and a Quarter. Two-fisted is not two-faced. Remember: One monkey don't stop no show. Let your fat belly be quilts of quietus. Pass on what the great winemakers know: The juice is not made in the vats but in the vincyard. Keep yourself rooted in the sun, rain, and darkly camphored air. Grow until you die, but before you do, leave your final kiss: Lay mint or orange eucalyptus garland, double tuck these lips. Careful to the very end what you deny, dismiss, & cut away.

I have spoken the best I know how.

Nikky Finney's Acceptance Speech for the National Book Award for Poetry

November 16, 2011 · Cipriani's, New York

We begin with history. The Slave Codes of South Carolina, 1739:

> *A fine of one hundred dollars and six months in prison will be imposed for anyone found teaching a slave to read or write, and death is the penalty for circulating any incendiary literature.*

The ones who longed to read and write, but were forbidden, who lost hands and feet, were killed by laws written by men who believed they owned other men. Their words devoted to quelling freedom and insurgency, imagination, all hope—what about the possibility of one day making a poem? The king's mouth and the queen's tongue arranged, to perfection, on the most beautiful paper, sealed with wax and palmetto tree sap, determined to control what can never be controlled: the will of the human heart to speak its own mind.

Tonight, these forbidden ones move all around the room as they please. They sit at whatever table they want. They wear camel-colored field hats and tomato-red kerchiefs. They are bold in their Sunday-go-to-meeting best. Their cotton croker-sack shirts are black washpot clean and irreverently not tucked in. Some have even come in white Victorian collars and bustiers. Some have just climbed out of the cold wet Atlantic, just to be here. We shiver together.

If my name is ever called out, I promised my girl-poet self, so too would I call out theirs.

Two:

Parneshia Jones (Acquisitions Editor), Marianne Jankowski (Art Director), and Northwestern University Press, this moment has everything to do with how seriously, how gorgeously, you do what you do.

A. J. Verdelle, editor-partner in this language life, you taught me that repetition is holy, Courage is a daughter's name, and two is stronger than one.

Papa, chief opponent of the death penalty in South Carolina for 50 years, 57 years married to the same Newberry girl, when I was a girl you bought every encyclopedia, dictionary, and Black history tome that ever knocked on our Oakland Avenue door.

Mama, dear Mama, Newberry girl, 57 years married to the same Smithfield boy, you made Christmas, Thanksgiving, and birthdays out of foil, lace, cardboard, and papier-mâché, insisting beauty into our deeply segregated southern days.

Adrienne Rich, Yusef Komunyakaa, Carl Phillips, and Bruce Smith, simply to be in your Finalist Company is to brightly burn.

National Book Foundation and 2011 National Book Award judges for poetry, there were special, and subversive, high school English teachers who would read and announce the highly anticipated annual report from the National Book Foundation, the names of the winners stowed way down deep in some dusty corner of our tiny southern newspaper.

Dr. Gloria Wade Gayles, great and best teacher, you asked me on a Friday, 4 o'clock, 1977, I was 19 and sitting on a Talladega College wall dreaming about the only life I ever wanted, that of a poet. "Miss Finney," you said, "do you really have time to sit there, have you finished reading every book in the library?"

Dr. Katie Cannon, what I heard you say once still haunts every poem I make: "Black people were the only people in the United States ever explicitly forbidden to become literate."

I am now, officially, speechless.

green
press
INITIATIVE

Northwestern University Press is committed to preserving ancient forests and natural resources. We elected to print this title on 30% post consumer recycled paper, processed chlorine free. As a result, for this printing, we have saved:

9 Trees (40' tall and 6-8" diameter)
4,150 Gallons of Wastewater
4 Million BTUs of Total Energy
263 Pounds of Solid Waste
921 Pounds of Greenhouse Gases

Northwestern University Press made this paper choice because our printer, Thomson-Shore, Inc., is a member of Green Press Initiative, a nonprofit program dedicated to supporting authors, publishers, and suppliers in their efforts to reduce their use of fiber obtained from endangered forests.

For more information, visit www.greenpressinitiative.org

Environmental impact estimates were made using the Environmental Defense Paper Calculator. For more information visit: www.papercalculator.org.